M000011365

Home Gardeners, Master Gardeners, Grounds Professionals, Golf Course Superintendents, and Green Committees take note when removing old overgrown or damaged trees from your property to allow sunlight and air movement, there are...

Desirable Trees
for the
Midwest

50 for the Home Landscape and Larger Properties

Scott A. Zanon

Copyright © 2009, Scott Zanon

All rights reserved. No part of this book may be reproduced or transmitted in any form or by any means, electronic or mechanical, including photocopying, recording, or by information storage and retrieval systems, without the written permission of the publisher, except by a reviewer who may quote brief passages in a review.

Printed in the United States of America

ISBN-13: 978-0-692-00348-0

Library of Congress Control Number: 2009927675

Contents

Foreword

Trees are a beautiful and natural part of North American golf courses and landscapes, but in most cases they have either been taken for granted or neglected. The problem isn't that we as golfers don't put a high value on trees, for we often over value them. Rather the problem is that we have not had good information sources, specific to golf courses, to refer to and rely on for selecting and caring for golf course trees. Until now that is.

Scott Zanon, senior author of this book, realized the lack of information on golf course trees as he served as Chair of the Scarlet Restoration Committee and on the Green Committee for The Ohio State University golf courses; 36 holes on 300-plus acres with lots of trees and tree issues. Typical of most golf courses, there were few trees on the OSU property when the golf courses were built in the 1930s. Then after World War II, seemingly everyone involved with the golf courses, to include golf course superintendents, golf staff, golf coaches, green committees, golfers, and university officials — felt compelled to instigate planting more trees. By the 1990s, it became clear that as many of the trees reached maturity, that they were either the wrong trees, or in the wrong place, or both, and were adversely affecting the golf course and golf experience. But once a tree reaches a certain size or stature, it becomes somewhat sacred to some people who subsequently resist its removal, no matter what the negative consequences it causes or potential liability it poses. Scott, who has a Bachelor of Science in Agriculture from The Ohio State University with majors in both Agronomy (turfgrass science) and Horticulture (landscape horticulture) took a more objective and balanced view of trees but faced stiff opposition when he proposed science-based reasons for tree renovations or removal. Furthermore, he really had no golf course specific information source he could use to convince folks what was the right thing to do. So he decided to collaborate with Horticulture professor Steve Still to write a user-friendly text to help others involved with trees in the home landscape and larger properties such as golf courses.

The result is a book that doesn't just look good on the book shelf; it also should become a well used source of information to improve the health and beneficial qualities of trees on golf courses and in the home landscape.

In school we are taught that a "weed" is any plant out of its proper place, and that includes trees. I have seen and experienced many instances where huge trees were simply "weeds" on the golf course. Perhaps the most dramatic example of that was a monster size silver maple that had perhaps a girth of 80"-90" that was growing on the fourth tee at Scioto Country Club. The tree not only degraded the turf on the tee through all of the normal negative influences of shade it produced, but it also had so many surface roots that it forced the green staff to more frequently hand water the tee to keep it uniformly green. In addition it posed a threat of wrist injury to golfers taking a divot. Furthermore the tree limited and was reducing the effective size of the tee, as well as greatly complicated the daily maintenance of the tee. That tree in another suitable location would have been revered but as it was, it was only loathed. Intellectually almost everyone agreed the tree was a significant problem that could only be solved by removal, but it was also emotionally difficult to allow it to happen. But, happen it did, and now the tee is so dramatically improved as is the entire golf hole, that almost no one misses or even mentions that tree, and wonders why it wasn't taken out long ago.

So put Scott's knowledge to work for you, and use his experience, intellect, and insights to make your golf course, large property, or home landscape better.

Sincerely,

Michael J. Hurdzan, Ph.D.
ASGCA
Hurdzan/Fry Environmental Golf Course Design

Preface

When I was asked to chair the Scarlet Restoration Committee at The Ohio State University Golf Club in 2003 by Director of Athletics Andy Geiger, little did I know that it would lead me to write this book.

We removed quite a few trees from the Scarlet Golf Course and I quickly realized there were no guides or writings listing desirable trees for use on golf courses. Naturally this crosses over into many other areas too.

With so many golf courses now taking out larger amounts of overgrown and poorly selected and site planted trees, it made sense that they have a re-planting program established with the idea to plant trees more suitable to the golf course but more importantly for the growth of turfgrass.

I have tried very hard to make this user-friendly to all readers whether it is golf course superintendents, golf course architects, green committees, horticulturists, arborists, grounds professionals, master gardeners, home gardeners, or homeowners.

Cultivars are listed but are not necessarily functionally better than the species. Cultivars are normally selected for marketing characteristics or purposes.

I sincerely hope this book is informative, useful, and educational for all of you. I also hope it provides thought and reason when selecting the desirable tree.

For additional copies of this book, please visit *www.DesirableTrees.com*.

Acknowledgments

This book would not be possible without the support and assistance of many special friends and people. It was a long journey; one that took longer than anticipated but nonetheless is very rewarding. Writing a book takes discipline and requires much patience.

I wish to thank Ohio State University Professor Emeritus Dr. Steven Still for his advice, guidance, and providing the majority of the photographs. I was privileged to have Steve, a true plantsman, as my instructor and mentor for all of the Horticulture identification classes at Ohio State consisting of woody plants, trees, shrubs, and perennials. He is currently Executive Director of the Perennial Plant Association.

I wish to thank Dr. Michael Hurdzan, ASGCA, for his encouragement to author this book. A noted and respected Golf Course Architect, Mike has received the Donald Ross Award from the American Society of Golf Course Architects. This award is given annually to a person who has made significant contributions to the game of golf and golf course architecture. It is the organization's highest honor.

I wish to thank Ohio State University Professor Dr. Karl Danneberger who thought I had a good idea that would be helpful when I approached him about writing this book. An Agronomist, Karl is a noted turfgrass expert in the Horticulture & Crop Science Department.

The following individuals and organizations helped in numerous ways from providing photographs and literature, sharing their knowledge and experience, and for allowing me to ask their advice. They are:

Dr. David Gardner — Associate Professor, Horticulture and Crop Science — The Ohio State University

Dr. Randall Heiligmann — Professor, School of Environment and Natural Resources — The Ohio State University

Doug Knaup — Horticulturist — The Ohio State University Golf Club

Robin Knaup — Willoway Nurseries

Mark Kroggel — University of Arizona

Dr. T. Davis Sydnor — Professor, Urban Forestry — School of Environment and Natural Resources — The Ohio State University

National Christmas Tree Association

U.S. National Arboretum

Mike Mignery — Photographic Creations

As beautiful as trees are, and as fond as you and I are of them, we still must not lose sight of the fact that there is a limited place for them in golf. We must not allow our sentiments to crowd out the real intent of a golf course, that of providing fair playing conditions. If it in any way interferes with a properly played stroke, I think the tree is an unfair hazard and should not be allowed to stand.

Donald Ross
Golf Has Never Failed Me

Trees Versus Turf
(an ongoing problem)

This has been an age-old battle that continues to be waged. Trees and turfgrass are plants each requiring different growing conditions, light requirements, nutrition requirements, and moisture needs.

Golf courses and homeowners across the country are beginning to pay attention to the turfgrass they so lovingly care for. One of the main culprits of poor turf growth is too much shade. Consequently many larger, older trees are being thinned, limbed-up, or simply removed. Trees and grasses do not mutually exist together. Grasses do not grow in the forests and trees do not flourish in the prairies. However, with some common sense and knowledge, they can peacefully coexist.

Problems occur when the care of trees and turf are not separated. Management requirements of each tend to compromise the other. Grass growing under a shade tree is usually weak, thin, and subject to weed invasion. Not an ideal situation, especially on a putting green where players expect perfect conditions. Putting surfaces need 8 hours of direct sunlight per day or thin turf with no tolerance for wear and tear will occur. Attempting to explain to a green committee the necessity of tree removal is a daunting task. Ecological tree removal often clashes with political and emotional issues. People in general do not like to cut down trees.

Shade from trees reduces turf quality and quantity. Light quality is the crucial issue. The green tree leaves filter the critical light wavelengths for photosynthesis. Turfgrass receives less light but also poorer light quality. Shade remains a major stress factor for turfgrass.

Shading is the main reason for poor turfgrass performance beneath trees. Reduced airflow and increased humidity levels may contribute to disease issues. An increase of air movement usually results in a decrease of diseases. Tree roots compete with grass for both water and nutrients. Root competition can promote stress but lack of light is the primary problem.

Morning shade has a great negative impact on turfgrass. Trees on the east and southeast sides of golf greens and properties create this morning shade. These areas do not receive the benefit of early morning sunlight and additionally dew does not evaporate quickly, thus extending cooler leaf and soil temperatures. Eliminate the morning shade issue by limbing-up, thinning, or by removing the entire tree. Trees that block morning sunlight must be considered for removal. Morning sun is more valuable than afternoon sun, so take heed.

Despite their differences, turf and trees can peacefully coexist and even thrive together. Achieving that balance can be attained. Armed with an understanding of how each affects the other, decisions can be reached regarding methods to modify the environment and maintenance procedures that will optimize the growing conditions for both. Good planning and proper tree selection is crucial.

Why Plant Trees?

Great question, isn't it? On the golf course, it is difficult to grow grass under them; they are the benefactor of most of the water and sunlight; their branching obstructs natural lines of sight and play yet with all of these problems, the mere mention or sound of a chainsaw elicits trepidation and panic. Mature trees can be problematic. All trees have their good and bad points. It is a rare occasion to find a tree that will make its owner happy over its lifespan.

Trees are integral components of both golf courses and landscapes. Imagine a golf course or yard without a tree. What a lonely expanse of nothingness that would be. Trees add grace and inspiration as well as architectural function. Trees can help a clubhouse or home be more energy efficient by providing shade, reflecting heat, and blocking cold winter winds.

Most human beings are tree-huggers by nature. We tend to become emotionally attached to them. Public courses and homeowners have the option to make decisions and actions about removing trees when they want. At private courses, members may freely protest any tree removal. Opposition is usually a sentimental rather than practical affair. Prior to the mid 1980s Golf Course Superintendents were told to leave beloved trees alone. This thought process has changed recently. Today's superintendent is charged with growing turfgrass of amazing quality and having fast greens, requiring consideration of tree management.

For far too long, golf courses gave little financial or planning consideration to trees. They ignored the possibility that old, mature trees planted 30–60 years ago could compete with turfgrass for water and sunlight. Decisions made long ago about what species to plant and the location of the planting rarely has any connection to the overall landscape or health of turfgrass. As these trees matured, the many attendant problems appeared. This is especially true when the green committee's dedication or tribute tree plantings are scattered haphazardly and with no rhyme nor reason throughout golf courses. When tree plantings overshadow the care of the turfgrass then a slow downward agronomic spiral begins.

With so many golf courses now taking out large numbers of trees, they are afforded the ability and opportunity to re-plant their golf course or property, not only with better consideration for locating the trees but using more suitable trees that also will help in the growth of turfgrass. Reducing competition among trees and selecting more desirable specimen or functional trees is a wonderful gift for others to appreciate in the future. There are many reasons for planting trees and it is important to have a specific purpose in mind. Overplanting is a costly error that affects future budgets. Focus on quality not quantity.

Since trees are a major element of a golf course, golf course superintendents must learn more about their care, form, and function. It is also imperative to maintain tree species diversity in case of catastrophic diseases like Dutch Elm or insect problems such as Emerald Ash Borer.

Climate change is happening because daily human activities emit exorbitant quantities of greenhouse gases (carbon dioxide emissions) into the global atmosphere. Trees are a tremendous biological means of sequestering carbon (CO^2) which helps offset fossil fuel emissions. They store carbon and are known as nature's "carbon sinks." So planting trees helps the environment too.

When planting a tree, enjoy its present but cherish it in its posterity. A tree can quickly outgrow its original purpose or can slowly grow into its intended one.

Selecting Trees

When selecting trees to plant, choose varieties that will not negatively impact greens, tees, fairways, property lines, and power lines when fully mature. Very simply: do the math. Find out what the mature size (height & width) will be of the tree and work backwards. Remember to not plant on the east or southeast sites where shade of the tree will ultimately cause problems. Before digging, be sure to contact your local utility company to mark gas lines, water pipes, or underground cables. The wrong tree species in the wrong location is a recipe for disaster for the turfgrass. Future tree removal is problematic and expensive.

From a golf course perspective, more often than not it makes sense to remove more trees than are planted each year. When purchasing new trees, disregard the end of the season close-out offerings from local nurseries. There usually is a reason no one else purchased these left-over trees: poor condition, deformed shape, ultra-common type, or not hardy to the area. Making that extra effort to purchase and plant high quality, desirable trees for a location will benefit all involved immensely. Select the tree based on your criteria and use the plant usage guides in this book to recommend viable options for you.

Form and habit should be considered before making a decision for your golf course or garden. Architectural structure is important especially during the winter months. Trees exhibiting an interesting shape or outline may still be appreciated when other plants are either dormant or dead. They may have weeping, arching, or sculpted branching. They may have dramatic or rounded canopies. They may be vase-shaped, pyramidal, or cascading. The appealing characteristic simply may be a massive trunk of a tree.

When selecting a tree to plant, habit is a wonderful characteristic to consider before making a decision. It is great to have all of the ornamental features, but a tree with appealing form and structure is appreciated throughout all seasons, plus it usually improves with age.

For golfers like me, we have all played a course where a majestic tree or a stand of trees served as a hazard. Often we likely cursed at them, spewing the invective that there was no reason for their existence in their present location. But after the tree's demise or removal, the view is altered and the challenge is instead now a collection of bunkers. One of my pet peeves is if a player hits the ball in a fairway then he or she deserves a clear shot at the green. My point is that moderation and common sense have to meet.

Trees may add a needed dimension architecturally to a golf course or property if properly selected, planted, and maintained. Great golf course and properties have reputations for their tree plantings. Comprehensive programs designed to care for existing trees and to plan properly for new plantings as they become necessary are vital.

Selective Pruning and Shade Seeding

Varying amounts of tree work is ongoing on practically every golf course and home property in spite of the inevitable backlash from everyone involved. Therefore, the best time to do selective pruning or tree removal is in the winter or during off-season, since it can be an emotional issue.

Selective pruning (while taking care not to ruin the shape of a tree of or shrub) allows most trees to remain on-site and helps allow enough sunlight through canopies for good turfgrass growth. Selective pruning increases air circulation which generally decreases humidity and disease problems.

Selective thinning will allow some light through. A great rule of thumb is to remove no more than ¼ of a tree's foliage crown in a single pruning. Limbing-up of trees or raising the canopy of trees that branch to the ground has proven to be a very effective method of pruning without affecting the beauty of the surrounding landscape. In fact, it usually enhances views. This procedure prunes lower limbs back to the trunk thus increasing airflow and decreasing shade.

Ultimately, however, one cannot prune enough to solve a serious shade issue. Sometimes trees just need to be removed. The problem is light quality, not light quantity. Most courses and properties that remove trees for the benefits of increased air circulation and sunlight will likely end up with some pretty great views too. Removing trees remove the problems but the best way to avoid the problem is thoughtful planning. Watch where you plant the trees.

Morning light is critical for turfgrass. Avoid planting trees on the east and south sides of tees and greens for golf courses and important turf locations like front or back yards. They block crucial morning sun so vital for optimum turfgrass growth. As turfgrass become hardier, healthier, and less prone to disease from increased sunlight, applications of fungicides, insecticides, and fertilizer will be reduced.

Fine-leaf fescues are considered the most shade tolerant of the cool-season grasses. They include creeping red fescue and chewings fescue. Turf-type tall fescue does well in moderate shade.

Fall seeding in shaded areas is preferred. The turf tends to be more successful as it enters the summer months with better root systems and more stored reserves of food.

Late fall fertilization of cool-season grasses is very beneficial in shaded environments. It really is the only time of the year when grass beneath the trees can effectively utilize the nitrogen without tree competition for nutrients, light, and moisture. Trees with shallow fibrous root systems compete fiercely with turfgrass for moisture.

If all else fails, then the planting of ground covers in heavily shaded areas is suggested. They look and work great.

Tree Cultural Practices

PLANTING: There are two ideal times to plant trees: fall (best) or early spring. However, planting the correct way can be the difference in a plant surviving the crucial first year. How the plant is packaged influences the condition of the roots which in turn determines how to put the tree in the ground to thrive.

There are 3 types of plant packaging: bare-root, container grown, and balled and burlapped (B&B).

Most mail-order catalogs ship purchased plants in bare-root form. These are harvested from fields with no soil attached to the roots. They are very perishable and should be both purchased and planted prior to spring bud break. The advantage of bare-root plants is that they allow thorough inspection of the root system prior to planting.

After taking possession, one must keep bare-root plants damp being careful not to allow their roots to dry out prior to planting them. Even in their dormant state they are alive and require water to survive. Keep them out of direct sunlight too.

Now you have the ability to inspect and prune the roots prior to planting. With sharp pruners, remove all damaged and/or turned in roots. Clean cuts heal faster and decrease the chances of disease.

Dig a hole wide enough so roots can spread into their natural position. It must also be deep enough so the crown will be at or just above the soil line. Break up any soil clods to prevent air pockets and backfill half of the hole. Slowly water to settle the soil around the roots. Continue to backfill the hole and then water again to entirely settle the soil around the roots. Bare-root plants will initially require more frequent watering than container or B&B.

The most popular option for consumers is container grown plants. They are grown above the ground in a pot not filled with real soil but an artificial medium which leads to much easier handling.

Regardless of the material, remove and discard the container prior to planting. Inspect the roots. Gently loosen the whitish colored roots from the surface of the soil ball (but do not remove). This allows expansion of the roots into the new soil site and is imperative for the tree's survival.

Again with sharp pruners, cut out woody, thick roots to prevent girdling the trunk. The flow of water and food is greatly decreased throughout the plant if girdling occurs. If the plant is root-bound, use a sharp knife to slice it from top to bottom in 3-4 spots careful to make them 2-3" deep. In a healthy plant, new roots will sprout from these cuts.

Dig a hole 2-3 times wider than the container which allows emerging roots to expand horizontally into the loose soil. Allow the crown of the tree to be slightly above grade level. Set the plant and backfill halfway then water to settle the soil. Finish backfilling and water again to settle the rest of the soil. At this point many commonly use their feet to tamp the soil but all it really does is promote compaction and should be avoided.

Larger trees and shrubs typically are sold balled and burlapped (B&B). B&B plants are field dug with a ball of soil wrapped in burlap which surrounds the roots. They are mainly available at nurseries and the weight of them makes them cumbersome to work with. That being said, larger plants are often only available in this form.

Dig a hole 2-3 times wider than the root-ball which allows emerging roots to expand horizontally into the loose soil near the soil surface where more oxygen is present. Make sure the root-ball top sits just above the soil grade.

After the plant is placed properly in the hole, backfill halfway and water to reduce air pocket development. This will also assist in stabilizing the plant. Contrary to popular belief, remove all wire or rope tied around the main trunk and remove the burlap from the top of the root-ball. The burlap on the bottom of the root-ball will decompose and disintegrate as the roots grow through it and expand.

Backfill and attempt to break up large clods of soil preventing air pockets. Construct a raised berm around the outside planting hole. Do not place extra soil on top of the root-ball. Gently water inside of the berm allowing the soil to settle around the root-ball. Again, do not use your feet to tamp the area as it will promote compaction.

WATERING: 1" of water per week during the first year is a good guide. In our northern climate, irrigate until the ground freezes. During dry periods, water established trees every 10-14 days.

MYCORRHIZAL FUNGI: This soil treatment (supplement) for trees is a standard part of re-forestry practices in most areas of the world and has been around since the 1850s. Co-existing with trees and plants in nature, these beneficial fungi provide a safety net for the tree in times of stress. By colonizing the roots and extending themselves further into the soil, the fungi enable the tree to absorb more nutrients and moisture resulting in a healthier tree better capable of tolerating stressful conditions.

FERTILIZING: New plantings should not be fertilized during the first year. For established plants, in the early spring use a complete fertilizer at a rate of two pounds per 1" of trunk diameter. Apply a second application at the same rate in late summer. An easy and effective way to apply the granular fertilizer is with a broadcast spreader.

MULCHING: A layer of mulch (3-4") around newly planted or established trees helps maintain soil moisture, smothers weeds, regulates temperature, and protects from the dreaded trimmer or lawnmower trunk damage (lawn mower blight).

PRUNING: Inspect your new planting and remove any broken, dead, or diseased limbs. Wait 1-2 years before beginning to train and shape. Use selective pruning for established trees as needed to maintain size, shape, and to encourage growth, flowering, and fruiting. Most plants respond favorably to late winter or early spring pruning. It is also easier to see what needs to be pruned with the absence of leaves. Remember, though, to prune spring blooming plants right after they flower, not before, or none will exist.

STAKING: Proper staking is to prevent the root-ball from rocking and not to prevent the top of the tree from being blown by the wind. A stable root-ball is necessary for good root development. Almost all staking should be removed after one year and many times is not even warranted.

List of 50 Desirable Trees

Deciduous Trees

1. Acer buergerianum---Trident Maple
2. Acer griseum---Paperbark Maple
3. Acer rubrum---Red Maple; Swamp Maple
4. Acer saccharum---Sugar Maple; Rock Maple; Hard Maple
5. Aesculus octandra---Yellow Buckeye
6. Aesculus parviflora---Bottlebrush Buckeye
7. Aesculus pavia---Red Buckeye
8. Amelanchier sp.---Serviceberry; Juneberry; Shadbush; Shadblow, etc.
9. Betula nigra---River Birch
10. Carpinus betulus---European Hornbeam; Common Hornbeam
11. Cercis canadensis---Eastern Redbud
12. Chionanthus virginicus---White Fringetree
13. Cladrastis kentuckea---American Yellowwood
14. Cornus florida---Flowering Dogwood
15. Cornus kousa---Kousa Dogwood; Chinese Dogwood
16. Cornus mas---Corneliancherry Dogwood
17. Fagus sylvatica---European Beech
18. Ginkgo biloba---Ginkgo; Maidenhair Tree
19. Gleditsia triacanthos var. inermis---Thornless Honeylocust
20. Gymnocladus dioicus---Kentucky Coffeetree
21. Koelreuteria paniculata---Panicled Goldenraintree; Varnish Tree
22. Liriodendron tulipifera---Tuliptree; Tulip Poplar; Yellow Poplar

23. Magnolia acuminata---Cucumbertree Magnolia; Cucumber Magnolia
24. Magnolia stellata---Star Magnolia
25. Magnolia virginiana---Sweetbay Magnolia; Laurel Magnolia
26. Malus sp.---Flowering Crabapple
27. Nyssa sylvatica---Black Tupelo; Black Gum; Sour Gum
28. Parrotia persica---Persian Parrotia; Persian Ironwood
29. Quercus acutissima---Sawtooth Oak
30. Quercus bicolor---Swamp White Oak
31. Quercus imbricaria---Shingle Oak; Laurel Oak
32. Quercus palustris---Pin Oak
33. Quercus rubra---Red Oak; Northern Red Oak; Eastern Red Oak
34. Quercus shumardii---Shumard Oak
35. Sassafras albidum---Common Sassafras
36. Syringa reticulata---Japanese Tree Lilac
37. Tilia cordata---Littleleaf Linden
38. Tilia tomentosa---Silver Linden
39. Ulmus americana---American Elm (resistant cultivars)
40. Ulmus parviflora---Lacebark Elm; Chinese Elm
41. Ulmus x Frontier---Frontier Elm
42. Zelkova serrata---Japanese Zelkova

Coniferous Trees

1. Abies balsamea var. phanerolepis---Canaan Fir
2. Juniperus virginiana---Eastern Redcedar
3. Metasequoia glyptostroboides---Dawn Redwood (Deciduous)
4. Picea omorika---Serbian Spruce
5. Picea orientalis---Oriental Spruce
6. Pinus bungeana---Lacebark Pine
7. Pinus strobus---Eastern White Pine
8. Taxodium distichum---Common Baldcypress (Deciduous)

Tree Growth Rates Table

Slow < 12"/year

Medium 12-24"/year

Fast > 24"/year

Individual List by Scientific Name
with Photographs

Scientific Name: *Acer buergerianum*

Hardiness Zones: 5-9

Mature Size: 20-30' tall & wide

Habit: Oval-rounded

Growth Rate: Slow

Bark: Gray-brown-orange; exfoliating with age; good winter interest

Leaf Color: Glossy dark green

Fall Color: Yellow-red-purple but late and variable

Flowers: Green-yellow in April but inconspicuous

Fruit: Samara

Disease & Insect Problems: None serious

Culture: Prefers well-drained acid soil; full sun; displays good drought resistance

Recommended Cultivars (if any):

Author Notes: This single-trunked small shade tree is a handsome addition to any area and is underutilized. The 3-lobed leaf is unusual as it look like a duck's foot. In certain years the tree can produce a heavy fruit set of samaras which could clutter annual or perennial beds and present problems later of germination.

Common Name(s):

Paperbark Maple

Scientific Name: *Acer griseum*

Hardiness Zones: 5-8

Mature Size: 20-30' tall x 15' wide

Habit: Upright oval

Growth Rate: Slow

Bark: Peeling cinnamon-exfoliating-visually striking

Leaf Color: Dark blue-green trifoliate leaf

Fall Color: Bronze-red late; often October and November

Flowers: Green in May but not ornamental

Fruit: Samara

Disease & Insect Problems: None serious

Culture: Prefers well-drained, moist acid soil; adaptable to clay soil; full sun to partial shade

Recommended Cultivars (if any):

Author Notes: A true specimen, this small ornamental tree has unrivaled aesthetic qualities. It is somewhat expensive but worth the splendor of its year-round appeal. Have patience for its slow growth as the reward is outstanding. A 4-season plant.

21

Scientific Name: *Acer rubrum*

Hardiness Zones: 3-9

Mature Size: 70' tall x 40' wide; 'Cultivars' smaller

Habit: Pyramidal to elliptical

Growth Rate: Medium-fast

Bark: Soft gray to gray-brown

Leaf Color: Emerging red-tinged the becoming medium-dark green

Fall Color: Green-yellow to yellow to red; 'Cultivars' best for fall color

Flowers: Red and noticeable before foliage; March-April

Fruit: Samara

Disease & Insect Problems: Leaf scorch and Verticillium wilt but not common

Culture: Tolerant of many soils and pH levels; will tolerate wet soil; full to partial sun; shows manganese deficiency (chlorosis) in high pH soil

Recommended Cultivars (if any):
    'Autumn Flame'---smaller leaf; red fall color 2 weeks earlier than species
    'Autumn Spire'---columnar; scarlet fall color
    'October Glory'---rounded; crimson fall color lasting 3 weeks
    'Red Rocket'---new release; cold hardy and intense red fall color
    'Franksred' (Red Sunset®)---upright; outstanding orange-red fall color
    'Somerset'---new release; stunning red fall color; October Glory x Autumn Flame
    'Sun Valley'---new release; long lasting dark red fall color; Red Sunset x Autumn Flame

Author Notes: Straight species is a large shade tree. 'Cultivars' would be considered a medium common shade and autumn accent tree and are preferred. An excellent specimen tree and valued for relatively quick growth, good shade, and its elegant symmetry in youth. Surface roots can be a concern.

Common Name(s):
Sugar Maple
Rock Maple
Hard Maple

Scientific Name: *Acer saccharum*

Hardiness Zones: 4-8

Mature Size: 60-80' tall x 40' wide

Habit: Upright oval to rounded

Growth Rate: Medium

Bark: Smooth gray-brown becoming furrowed with age; irregular plates

Leaf Color: Medium-dark green

Fall Color: Yellow-orange-red and striking

Flowers: Green-yellow in April but not showy

Fruit: Samara

Disease & Insect Problems: Leaf scorch in droughty conditions; Verticillium wilt

Culture: Prefers well-drained, moist fertile soil; full sun; very adaptable to pH levels; can be difficult to establish; frost cracking sometimes a problem

Recommended Cultivars (if any):
'Adirondak'---pyramidal; golden orange fall color 2 weeks earlier than species
'Commemoration'---deep yellow-orange-red fall color 2 weeks earlier than species
'Goldspire'---columnar; bright yellow-orange fall color
'Legacy'---fast grower; yellow to orange-red fall color
'Wright Brothers'---fast grower; fall color tends to be more red

Author Notes: This stately large shade tree is one of the best. It may be used as a specimen or autumn accent tree. Some cultivars available for excellent fall color. Overall it is generally thought of as a poor urban selection.

Yellow Buckeye

Scientific Name: *Aesculus octandra*

Hardiness Zones: 3-8

Mature Size: 60-75' tall x 40' wide

Habit: Upright oval

Growth Rate: Medium

Bark: Gray-brown with large, flat, smooth plates

Leaf Color: Dark green

Fall Color: Pumpkin orange to yellow-brown

Flowers: Yellow inflorescence in mid-May

Fruit: Smooth pear shaped capsule splitting in October to yield 2 brown nuts

Disease & Insect Problems: None serious

Culture: Prefers deep, moist, well-drained soil along with full to partial shade

Recommended Cultivars (if any):

Author Notes: A stately, handsome large shade tree preferable to the Ohio Buckeye (Aesculus glabra). It is considered to be the best large buckeye tree.

27

Common Name(s):

Bottlebrush Buckeye

Scientific Name: *Aesculus parviflora*

Hardiness Zones: 4-8

Mature Size: 10' tall & wide

Habit: Wide-spreading multi-stemmed mound

Growth Rate: Slow but suckers (basal) grow quickly and require pruning

Bark: Ash gray

Leaf Color: Dark green and drooping form

Fall Color: Yellow-green to yellow-brown to clear yellow which can be outstanding

Flowers: White extending 1" beyond petals (bottlebrush-like) in July; usually a stunning 2-week show on 10" long x 3" wide inflorescences

Fruit: Light brown smooth capsule

Disease & Insect Problems: None serious

Culture: Prefers well-drained moist soil; pH adaptable; full sun to partial shade

Recommended Cultivars (if any):

Author Notes: A sprawling multi-stemmed medium shrub/small tree. Excellent for massing, border, specimen and can be used under shade trees or shade beds. A superb understory plant that is finally becoming more recognized and available.

Scientific Name: *Aesculus pavia*

Hardiness Zones: 4-8

Mature Size: 10-20' tall & wide

Habit: Rounded

Growth Rate: Slow-medium

Bark: Light brown and smooth in youth becoming flaky and attractive with age

Leaf Color: Dark green

Fall Color: Yellow-brown and early drop in late September

Flowers: Showy red 6" panicles in May; attract hummingbirds

Fruit: Smooth, round tan capsules

Disease & Insect Problems: Some leaf scorch in hot, dry summers possible

Culture: Ideally suited in partial shade to full sun; prefers moist, well-drained soil

Recommended Cultivars (if any):
'Atrosanguinea'---deeper red flowers
'Humilus'---low or prostrate shrub with red flowers in small panicles

Author Notes: This handsome small ornamental tree in flower makes a fine specimen. Since it does drop its leaves early, place around other plants and let its branches provide a coarse architectural interest. Found as single- or multi-trunked forms.

Common Name(s):
Serviceberry
Juneberry
Shadbush
Shadblow
Saskatoon
Sarvisberry

Scientific Name: *Amelanchier sp.*

Hardiness Zones: 4-9

Mature Size: 6-30' tall x 4-10' wide; 12' tall x 10' wide-cultivars

Habit: Upright oval

Growth Rate: Slow-medium

Bark: Gray and smooth; striped when older; ornamental feature

Leaf Color: Medium green

Fall Color: Yellow to orange to red in October often in spectacular fashion

Flowers: Showy white in mid-April

Fruit: Purple-black at maturity and edible (sweet); ripens in June; robins and squirrels often devour the fruit; Species is a commercial fruit tree in Canada

Disease & Insect Problems: None serious

Culture: Prefers moist, rich, well-drained soils; full sun to partial shade; very adaptable

Recommended Cultivars (if any):
   Amelanchier alnifolia (Saskatoon Serviceberry) 'Regent'---mounding compact type
   Amelanchier canadensis (Shadblow Serviceberry) 'Glennform' (Rainbow Pillar®)---upright columnar
      habit suggesting use as screen or hedge
   Amelanchier x grandiflora (Apple Serviceberry) 'Autumn Brilliance'---profuse flowering and bright
      red fall color; hybrid of Downy and Allegheny; fast grower
   Amelanchier laevis (Allegheny Serviceberry) 'Lamarckii'---cultivar that is somewhat smaller and has
      an upright growth habit
   'Cumulus'---vigorous upright growth habit with orange-red fall color; good street tree

Author Notes: One of the best 4-season small-medium ornamental trees that is available either multi- or single-trunked. It functions well in a naturalistic setting or as a specimen. There are many species and cultivars to choose from. Author prefers <u>Amelanchier laevis</u> but all are fabulous selections.

Scientific Name: *Betula nigra*

Hardiness Zones: 3-9

Mature Size: 40-60' tall x 40' wide

Habit: Upright oval

Growth Rate: Medium-fast

Bark: Exfoliating papery sheets of white, black, cinnamon, and cream shades

Leaf Color: Lustrous medium-dark green

Fall Color: Yellow

Flowers: Catkins

Fruit: Small nutlet in spring

Disease & Insect Problems: None serious & highly resistant to bronze birch borer

Culture: Performs best in moist soils with pH of ↓ 6.5 or chlorosis may occur; full to partial sun; will tolerate dry soils

Recommended Cultivars (if any):
'Cully' (Heritage®)---larger leaved, more exfoliation, and outstanding bark color
'Little King'---dwarf
'Shiloh Slash'---variegated foliage
'Duraheat'---heat-tolerant
'Summer Cascade'---pendulous, smaller cultivar reaching 10-20' height
'Fox Valley'---compact, smaller cultivar reaching mature height of 10-20'

Author Notes: This large, fine-textured shade tree is also considered an ornamental because of its peeling bark. Some chlorosis may occur in high pH soils. Available as a multi-trunked form of 3-5 trunks, this fine specimen tree is perfect for areas along streams or ponds. A 4-season plant.

Common Name(s):
European Hornbeam
Common Hornbeam

Scientific Name: *Carpinus betulus*

Hardiness Zones: 4-7

Mature Size: 40' tall x 30' wide

Habit: Pyramidal to oval-rounded

Growth Rate: Medium

Bark: Ornamental, smooth and slate gray; fluted; muscle-like

Leaf Color: Dark green

Fall Color: Yellow to yellow-green and late

Flowers: Pendulous catkins in April

Fruit: Light brown nutlet in October

Disease & Insect Problems: None serious

Culture: Tolerant of many soil conditions but must be well-drained; full sun

Recommended Cultivars (if any):
 'Fastigiata'---upright growth; effective for screens and hedging
 'Franz Fontaine'---unique central leader with in-ward curving branches; maintains fastigiate form
     with maturity
 'Globosa'---slow growing rounded form 5' x 12'
 'Pendula'---weeping pendulous branching

Author Notes: A fine medium-sized specimen tree noted for its dense foliage providing great symmetry and architectural value. Also excellent for effective year-round screens or hedges as it withstands pruning.

Scientific Name: *Cercis canadensis*

Hardiness Zones: 4-9

Mature Size: 15-25' tall & wide

Habit: Upright-vase shaped

Growth Rate: Fast in youth then slowing to medium

Bark: Somewhat ornamental with orange inner bark and brown-black outer bark

Leaf Color: Emerging red-purple and changing to dark green; heart-shaped

Fall Color: Yellow-green to yellow

Flowers: Bright lavender in April before leaves emerge

Fruit: Brown pod 2-3" long in October

Disease & Insect Problems: Canker is most destructive disease; some verticillium wilt

Culture: Prefers moist, well-drained soil; does not tolerate wet feet; adaptable to pH; full sun to partial shade

Recommended Cultivars (if any):
   var. alba---white flowers
   'Covey' (Lavender Twist™)---weeping umbrella-like crown
   'Forest Pansy'---leaves emerge red-purple; rose-purple flowers; some damage in cold winters
   'Texas White'---white flowers with a more compact head

Author Notes: A popular, small ornamental tree with showy spring flowers. Best for naturalized, woodland (understory) settings. Unfortunately this is not a long-lived tree as the life span is 15-20 years.

39

Common Name(s):
White Fringetree

Scientific Name: *Chionanthus virginicus*

Hardiness Zones: 3-9

Mature Size: 10-20' tall & wide

Habit: Spreading with variable shapes

Growth Rate: Slow

Bark: Smooth gray in youth becoming slightly furrowed

Leaf Color: Medium green; extremely late to leaf out (mid-May)

Fall Color: Yellow to brown

Flowers: White, slight fragrance after foliage expands; fleecy, drooping 6-8" panicles in late-May to early-June; outstanding

Fruit: Dark blue drupe ripening in September and prized by animals; dioecious so fruit is only on females; plant 1 male to 5 female

Disease & Insect Problems: None serious

Culture: Prefers deep moist, acidic soil but is adaptable; full sun to partial shade

Recommended Cultivars (if any):

Author Notes: One of the best small native American flowering plants. Commonly multi-trunked this can be pruned to a single stem form and makes a great specimen tree/shrub. Great for naturalized areas as a group or border planting preferring afternoon shade.

Common Name(s):
American
Yellowwood

Scientific Name: *Cladrastis kentuckea (lutea)*

Hardiness Zones: 4-8

Mature Size: 30-50' tall & wide

Habit: Rounded vase with low branching

Growth Rate: Medium

Bark: Thin, gray and resembling beech; beautiful

Leaf Color: Opening bright yellow-green and gradually turning to bright green

Fall Color: Yellow to golden yellow

Flowers: White (long panicles), fragrant, and ornamental in June

Fruit: Tan-brown pod in October

Disease & Insect Problems: None serious

Culture: Best in full sun and likes well-drained soil; adaptable to pH

Recommended Cultivars (if any):
    'Rosea'---pink flowers

Author Notes: This choice medium ornamental shade tree is excellent as a specimen or in groupings. Flowers attract bees and prune only in the summer as it is a profuse bleeder. Problematic bad crotches that can split in wind storms.

Flowering Dogwood

Scientific Name: *Cornus florida*

Hardiness Zones: 5-9

Mature Size: 15' tall x 20' wide

Habit: Upright oval with low-branching and horizontal spread

Growth Rate: Slow

Bark: Gray to dark brown with small rectangular blocks

Leaf Color: Medium-dark green

Fall Color: Red to purple

Flowers: Inconspicuous green-yellow; white bracts are showy in May

Fruit: Glossy red drupe ripening in October; birds love to devour

Disease & Insect Problems: Many including borer, anthracnose, and powdery mildew

Culture: Prefers acid, well-drained site to maintain cool, moist soil; best in partial shade

Recommended Cultivars (if any):

'Cherokee Chief'---red-pink flowers; foliage emerges red then becomes green
'Cherokee Sunset'---red flowers; foliage emerges green with dark pink margin, changing to a creamy
    margin; pink-purple fall color; resistant to anthracnose
'Cloud Nine'---large white flowers; red fall color
'Welchii'---white flowers; variegated foliage with pink-purple fall colors

Author Notes: An aristocratic small tree with 4-season appeal. It tends to be short-lived in urban areas due to adaptation issues like alkaline and dry soils. This is a native understory tree that is best used as a specimen or in groupings. The pink and red "flower" selections are usually not cold hardy.

45

Common Name(s):
Kousa Dogwood
Chinese Dogwood

Scientific Name: *Cornus kousa*

Hardiness Zones: 5-8

Mature Size: 20-25' tall & wide

Habit: Vase shape in youth becoming rounded with age

Growth Rate: Slow

Bark: Mottled cream-gray with some exfoliation

Leaf Color: Dark blue-green

Fall Color: Burgundy in late autumn

Flowers: Inconspicuous; bracts are creamy white in June

Fruit: Pink-red raspberry-like drupe in September-October

Disease & Insect Problems: None serious

Culture: Adaptable to varying soil pH; prefers well-drained soil doing best in full sun but can take partial shade

Recommended Cultivars (if any):

var. chinensis 'Milky Way'---amazing flower and fruit production versus species
'Elizabeth Lustgarten'---weeping mainly on upper branches; distinctive
'Moonbeam'---large 7-8" flowers on long peduncles at eye level
'Satomi'---pink-red bracts
'Wolf Eyes'---white margined leaves with impressive pink-red fall color
Cornus 'Rutcan' Constellation™---long white bracts
Cornus 'Rutgan' Stellar Pink™---rounded soft-pink bracts

Author Notes: A handsome small ornamental 4-season tree with layered branching. Kousa is more resistant to drought than Flowering Dogwood. Use as a specimen or seasonal accent tree. Many cultivars are available in the trade. There are new hybrids of *C. kousa* x *C. florida* developed at Rutgers University by Dr. Elwin Orton which seem to be resistant to dogwood borer and anthracnose and are more vigorous and erect.

Corneliancherry Dogwood

Scientific Name: *Cornus mas*

Hardiness Zones: 4-8

Mature Size: 20' tall & wide

Habit: Oval-rounded

Growth Rate: Medium

Bark: Exfoliating, flaky with gray-brown colors

Leaf Color: Dark green and glossy

Fall Color: Variable, can be purple-red but leaves may drop green too in late fall

Flowers: Yellow in March before leaves; a sign that spring has arrived

Fruit: Bright cherry-red oblong drupe in July; have seen the fruit used for jelly, jam, and to make wine

Disease & Insect Problems: None serious

Culture: Adaptable to varying soil types and pH; best in well-drained rich soil; full sun to partial shade

Recommended Cultivars (if any):
   'Golden Glory'---more upright and profuse flowering than species; purple-red fall color
   'Redstone'---abundant large red fruit
   'Variegata'---showy bark; variegated white-green foliage; red fall color

Author Notes: An excellent small ornamental tree or large ornamental shrub. A very durable and underutilized dogwood, it is typically multi-trunked with branching close to the ground. It is effective as a screen, hedge, or border and superb as an early spring flowering specimen.

Scientific Name: *Fagus sylvatica*

Hardiness Zones: 4-7

Mature Size: 50-60' tall & 35-45' wide

Habit: Upright oval

Growth Rate: Slow

Bark: Smooth, gray and darker than American Beech; ornamental in winter

Leaf Color: Shimmering green changing to dark green; emerges late

Fall Color: Golden bronze

Flowers: April-May with leaves

Fruit: Triangular nuts in 4-lobed spiny husks; October

Disease & Insect Problems: Few

Culture: Ideally suited in full sun to part-shade; prefers deep well-drained soil

Recommended Cultivars (if any):
   'Asplenifolia'---cut leaves that turn golden brown fall color
   'Pendula'---graceful weeping
   'Tricolor'---outstanding purple foliage with irregular cream and rose borders

Author Notes: It would be difficult to find a finer specimen tree. This large, graceful 4-season shade tree is more tolerant of compacted soils than American Beech although there may be some surface roots with age. It naturally branches close to the ground. There are many cultivars to pick from for growth habit and varied foliage.

Scientific Name: *Ginkgo biloba*

Hardiness Zones: 4-8

Mature Size: 60-80' tall & 40-60' wide

Habit: Upright columnar

Growth Rate: Slow-medium

Bark: Gray-brown with dark furrows; distinctive and handsome

Leaf Color: Bright green and fan-shaped

Fall Color: Yellow in November and one of the finest

Flowers: Green; March-April; catkins

Fruit: Naked seed; fleshy covering and rank odor; female trees

Disease & Insect Problems: None

Culture: Prefers deep sandy soil but adaptable to stressful situations and pH levels

Recommended Cultivars (if any):
  'Autumn Gold'---non-fruiting; symmetrical; golden fall color
  'Princeton Sentry'---columnar; upright
  'Saratoga'---non-fruiting; distinct central leader

Author Notes: An excellent large shade tree that is very urban tolerant and bold textured. Be patient, will evolve into a spectacular specimen or focal point tree. A gymnosperm, making it one of the oldest trees growing on earth, it is recommended to purchase and plant male species only.

53

Scientific Name: *Gleditsia triacanthos var. inermis*

Hardiness Zones: 4-9

Mature Size: 60' tall x 40' wide

Habit: Upright oval

Growth Rate: Fast

Bark: Gray-brown with vertical fissures

Leaf Color: Bright green

Fall Color: Yellow; drop early in autumn

Flowers: Green-yellow in May-June; slightly fragrant and nectar laden

Fruit: Long pods; red-brown-black in fall

Disease & Insect Problems: Numerous problems including canker, rust, borer, webworm

Culture: Tolerant of a wide range of conditions including drought and high pH; full sun; very urban tolerant

Recommended Cultivars (if any):
'Christie' (Halka™)---rounded and broad with bright green leaves; fast-growing
'Emerald Kascade'---irregular weeping; seedless; dark green foliage
'Impcole' (Imperial®)---spreading habit with bright green leaves
'Skycole' (Skyline®)---pyramidal with bright yellow fall color
'Suncole' (Sunburst®)---pyramidal; new growth golden yellow turning to bright green

Author Notes: One of the most adaptable large trees that provides filtered summer shade and minimal leaf litter. Surface roots can be a problem and always prune in the fall. Provides a beautiful winter outline but is somewhat overused and has a few problems.

Scientific Name: *Gymnocladus dioicus*

Kentucky Coffeetree

Hardiness Zones: 3-8

Mature Size: 60-75' tall x 40-50' wide

Habit: Irregular growth in youth becoming upright rounded

Growth Rate: Slow-medium

Bark: Rough; gray-brown to dark brown scaly plates

Leaf Color: Emerging purple tinged then becoming dark green; late to leaf out; mid-May

Fall Color: Ineffective; some yellow

Flowers: White-green in late May to early June

Fruit: Leathery pods; red-brown in October and tend to hang on through winter

Disease & Insect Problems: None serious

Culture: Best in deep, rich, moist soils but very adaptable; full sun

Recommended Cultivars (if any):

Author Notes: A choice large tree with semi-filtered shade and a beautiful, bold winter canopy. Older trees are majestic and handsome. It can get somewhat dirty with the pods and leaflets and prune only in winter/early spring. This tree is dioecious so the males do not fruit.

Scientific Name: *Koelreuteria paniculata*

Hardiness Zones: 5-9

Mature Size: 30' tall & wide

Habit: Upright rounded

Growth Rate: Medium-fast

Bark: Light gray-brown with furrows as tree ages

Leaf Color: Emerging purple-toned then turning bright green

Fall Color: Inconsistent but some yellow-yellow orange

Flowers: Showy yellow 12-15" panicles in early July

Fruit: 3-sided brown pods about 2" long containing 1-3 round black seeds; may persist through winter

Disease & Insect Problems: None serious

Culture: Very adaptable to soil conditions; withstands drought; full sun

Common Name(s):
Panicled
Goldenraintree
Varnish Tree

Recommended Cultivars (if any):

Author Notes: This medium ornamental or shade tree is unrivaled for yellow flowers in summer months and its urban tolerance. Excellent street trees as there are two in my front yard.

59

Scientific Name: *Liriodendron tulipifera*

Hardiness Zones: 4-9

Mature Size: 70-90' tall x 35-50' wide

Habit: Pyramidal to oval-rounded

Growth Rate: Fast

Bark: In youth, smooth and gray; develops deep furrows with age and easily recognized

Leaf Color: Green and somewhat glossy; unique 4-lobed shape

Fall Color: Yellow-golden yellow in October to early November

Flowers: 6 beautiful green-yellow petals in mid-May to mid-June

Fruit: Cone-like samaras 2-3" long that turn brown in October and persist through winter

Disease & Insect Problems: Several minor insect and disease problems, notably aphids causing some cosmetic issues

Culture: Prefers deep, moist, well-drained loamy soil; full sun; pH adaptable; prune in winter

Recommended Cultivars (if any):

Author Notes: A large fast-growing shade tree with showy tulip-like flowers which usually begin at 15 years of age. It is one of the largest shade trees with a strong central leader. Exceptional when planted in large groupings or groves. Twig and small branch litter are messy especially in small yards.

Scientific Name: *Magnolia acuminata*

Hardiness Zones: 3-8

Mature Size: 50-70' tall & wide

Habit: Pyramidal in youth to rounded at maturity

Growth Rate: Medium-fast

Bark: Smooth gray-brown in youth; ridged and furrowed with age

Leaf Color: Dark green and large

Fall Color: Not exciting but a few will exhibit a soft ash-brown

Flowers: Green-yellow petals in May to early June; slightly fragrant

Fruit: Pink-red in October resembling 2-3" small cucumber

Disease & Insect Problems: None serious

Culture: Prefers deep, loamy, well-drained soils; performs well in the calcareous soils of the Midwest; partial shade-full sun; not tolerable of extreme drought or wetness

Recommended Cultivars (if any):
   'Koban Dori'---pale yellow flowers typically on older trees

Author Notes: This is an excellent large shade tree and provides great character for large properties such as a golf course. It is the hardiest of the native Magnolia species. Nursery grown cultivars have showy yellow flowers and are becoming easier to find in the nursery trade.

Common Name(s):
Star Magnolia

Scientific Name: *Magnolia stellata*

Hardiness Zones: 4-8

Mature Size: 15-20' tall & wide

Habit: Oval-rounded

Growth Rate: Slow

Bark: Gray, smooth, and handsome on mature plants

Leaf Color: Dark green

Fall Color: Green-yellow; not exciting

Flowers: White, slight fragrance in April before leaves

Fruit: Not distinguishable

Disease & Insect Problems: None serious

Culture: As with most magnolias, some form of protection is best; full sun to partial shade; tolerant of soil types and pH

Recommended Cultivars (if any):
'Royal Star'---earliest bloomer with pink buds opening to fragrant white flowers

Author Notes: A small, upright multi-trunked tree or shrub with showy white flowers that are frequently browned by early spring frosts. Used mainly as a specimen or accent tree.

Common Name(s):
Sweetbay Magnolia
Laurel Magnolia

Scientific Name: *Magnolia virginiana*

Hardiness Zones: 5-9

Mature Size: 10-20' tall x 15' wide

Habit: Upright oval

Growth Rate: Slow-medium

Bark: Light gray and smooth

Leaf Color: Dark green and elliptical

Fall Color: Yellow to yellow-brown

Flowers: Creamy white and wonderful lemon scent; 2-3" in May-June often continuing until September

Fruit: Dark red seeds 2" long ripening in September

Disease & Insect Problems: None serious

Culture: Prefers acidic soils; full sun to full shade and tolerant of wet soils

Recommended Cultivars (if any):
'Jim Wilson' (Moonglow®)---upright and taller; dark foliage
'Green Bay'---evergreen

Author Notes: An upright, small multi-trunked tree with graceful lateral branching. It is prone to chlorosis in calcareous soils. Offers scented flowers throughout summer. Sweetbay magnolia is a North America native.

Scientific Name: *Malus sp.*

Hardiness Zones: 4-8

Mature Size: 15-25' tall & wide

Habit: Various

Growth Rate: Medium

Bark: Smooth when young; lightly furrowed and often knotty with age

Leaf Color: Green to dark green

Fall Color: Usually insignificant

Flowers: White, pink, or red; typically single-flowered before foliage in April-May

Fruit: Red, orange, yellow, or green in showy clusters September-October; some persist into December

Disease & Insect Problems: Fireblight, cedar apple rust, and apple scab to name a few problems mainly on older cultivars that have been removed from sale; lead to premature defoliation and fruit drop

Culture: Adaptable to varying soils but good drainage is a must; pH adaptable; drought and heavy pruning tolerant

Recommended Cultivars (if any):

There are a wide range of modern cultivars available in the trade that has tolerance or resistance to most of the pests and diseases that plague crabapples. Some favorites:

'Adirondack'---vase; crimson buds; white flowers; red fruits
'Bob White'---spreading; pink buds; white flowers; yellow fruits
'Centurion'---upright; red buds; pink-red flowers; glossy red fruits
'Donald Wyman'---spreading; red-pink buds; white flowers; glossy bright red fruits
'Harvest Gold'---columnar to vase; red-pink buds; white flowers; gold fruits
'Prairifire'---upright spreading; crimson buds; red-purple flowers; red fruits
'Professor Sprenger'---upright spreading; pink buds; white flowers; orange fruits
'Profusion'---upright spreader; red buds; deep pink flowers; maroon fruits
'Red Jade'---weeping; deep pink buds; white flowers; red fruits
'Red Jewel'---rounded; white buds; white flowers; cherry red fruits
'Sargentii'---dwarf spreading cultivar; red buds; white flowers; red fruits
'Sentinel'---columnar oval; red buds; profuse light pink–white flowers; small red fruits
'Snowdrift'---rounded; pink buds; white flowers; orange-red fruits
'Strawberry Parfait'---erratic upright-spreading; pink buds; pink flowers; red fruits
'Sugar Tyme'---upright; pink buds; white flowers; red fruits

Author Notes: Small to medium spring flowering ornamental tree mainly used for specimens. Known for spectacular spring flowering, varied growth habits and sizes, autumn/winter fruits, and urban tolerance. Beware of basal suckers and water sprouts, crossing branches that require pruning to keep neat look and vigor, and winter fruit litter in non-lawn areas. In the Midwest, there is no finer small ornamental tree.

Scientific Name: *Nyssa sylvatica*

Hardiness Zones: 3-9

Mature Size: 30-50' tall x 20-30' wide

Habit: Pyramidal

Growth Rate: Slow-medium

Bark: Dark gray-brown with blocky (rectangular) appearance

Leaf Color: Dark green, shiny, and elliptical

Fall Color: Outstanding fluorescent yellow, orange, scarlet, and purple

Flowers: Not effective or ornamentally significant

Fruit: Oblong blue-black drupe in late September/early October; favorite of birds and squirrels

Disease & Insect Problems: Some leaf spot causing cosmetic damage

Culture: Best in deep, moist, well-drained acid soils; full sun to partial shade; fall prune

Recommended Cultivars (if any):
   'NXSXF' (Forum™)---red fall color

Author Notes: An excellent large shade tree mainly used as a specimen. One of the best and most consistent native trees for fall color but not to be planted in alkaline soils. Underutilized, it has lustrous dark green summer foliage with striking autumn color. There can be some variability in its growth habit as most are upright but a few cascade.

Common Name(s):
Persian Parrotia
Persian Ironwood

Scientific Name: *Parrotia persica*

Hardiness Zones: 5-8

Mature Size: 30' tall x 20' wide

Habit: Oval rounded

Growth Rate: Medium

Bark: Some exfoliation on older trunks exposing a mosaic of gray, brown, white, and green

Leaf Color: Unfolding red-purple then changing to a shiny dark green

Fall Color: Beautiful yellow to orange to scarlet colors when exposed to full sun

Flowers: Red stamens in April but insignificant

Fruit: Capsule; ornamentally ineffective

Disease & Insect Problems: None serious

Culture: Prefers well-drained, loamy soils; full sun to partial shade; tolerant of some high pH; extremely tolerant; prune in spring

Recommended Cultivars (if any):

Author Notes: One of the best specimen trees known for foliage, bark, and pest resistance. This is an outstanding small ornamental tree with few rivals. It is typically low branched. This fine plant should be used more extensively in landscapes, parks, and golf courses. A 4-season plant.

73

Scientific Name: *Quercus acutissima*

Sawtooth Oak

Hardiness Zones: 5-9

Mature Size: 40-50' tall & wide

Habit: Pyramidal in youth becoming rounded with age

Growth Rate: Medium-fast

Bark: Brown with deep furrows; cork-like appearance

Leaf Color: Dark glossy green with serrated bristle-like teeth

Fall Color: Clear yellow to golden yellow in November

Flowers: 3-4" catkins in early April

Fruit: Acorn

Disease & Insect Problems: None serious

Culture: Prefers acid, well-drained soil but is adaptable; may develop chlorosis in high pH soil; performs well in heat; full sun

Recommended Cultivars (if any):

Author Notes: This is a handsome, clean foliaged large shade tree. The new leaves emerge bright yellow in the spring and exude a radiant glow to entire tree. Another underutilized tree in the landscape and can be a prolific bearer of acorns. The flowers of oaks are noticeable but not ornamental.

Swamp White Oak

Scientific Name: *Quercus bicolor*

Hardiness Zones: 3-8

Mature Size: 50-60' tall & wide

Habit: Upright oval in youth becoming rounded with age

Growth Rate: Medium

Bark: Brown; notable flared bark feature exhibiting bold winter texture

Leaf Color: Dark green with white-green undersides

Fall Color: Moderate yellow to yellow-brown with an occasional red-purple

Flowers: Yellow-brown catkins in late April; insignificant

Fruit: Acorn

Disease & Insect Problems: None serious

Culture: Full sun in moist to wet deep acid soils; adaptable to dry soils

Recommended Cultivars (if any):

Author Notes: A large, rounded shade tree noted for bi-color foliage in the wind, ornamental bark, and its bold texture in the winter. This tree is also adaptable to wet or dry sites.

Common Name(s):
Shingle Oak
Laurel Oak

Scientific Name: *Quercus imbricaria*

Hardiness Zones: 4-8

Mature Size: 60' tall x 70' wide

Habit: Upright oval in youth becoming rounded and spreading with age

Growth Rate: Medium

Bark: Gray-brown with shallow furrows

Leaf Color: Glossy dark green with lobeless oblong leaves

Fall Color: Yellow-brown to russet brown; poor

Flowers: Yellow-brown catkins in late April

Fruit: Acorn (small)

Disease & Insect Problems: None serious

Culture: Prefers moist, rich, deep well-drained acid soil; full sun; adaptable to poor soils, dry soils, and varying pH levels

Recommended Cultivars (if any):

Author Notes: Large, spreading shade tree that performs well in dry sites. This tree is also very cold hardy and urban tolerant.

Scientific Name: *Quercus palustris*

Hardiness Zones: 4-8

Mature Size: 60-70' tall x 25-40' & wide; 100' tall in nature

Habit: Upright pyramidal

Growth Rate: Medium-fast

Bark: Gray-brown and smooth in youth but developing narrow and shallow furrows

Leaf Color: Glossy dark green

Fall Color: Bronze to crimson red

Flowers: Yellow-brown catkins in late April; insignificant

Fruit: Acorn (small)

Disease & Insect Problems: Galls sometimes a problem but not too serious

Culture: Shallow, fibrous root systems allows transplantability; tolerant of wet soils; best in moist, rich, acid well-drained soils; intolerant of high pH; full sun

Recommended Cultivars (if any):

Author Notes: Strongly pyramidal in youth, this is a very popular large shade tree that tolerates wet or dry sites. Characteristics include downswept lower branches and ascending upper branches. If planted in low pH (acid) soils, the tree can grow rapidly. Do not plant in high pH (alkaline) soils as iron chlorosis will be a major problem.

Scientific Name: *Quercus rubra*

Hardiness Zones: 4-8

Mature Size: 60-75' tall & wide

Habit: Upright oval in youth becoming rounded with age

Growth Rate: Medium-fast

Bark: Brown to black; ridged and furrowed

Leaf Color: Lustrous dark green

Fall Color: Russet red to bright red; sometimes disappointing

Flowers: Catkins in late April

Fruit: Acorn (large)

Disease & Insect Problems: None serious

Culture: Prefers acid, well-drained loamy soils; full sun; may get some chlorosis in high pH soils

Recommended Cultivars (if any):
   'Splendens'---exhibits excellent red fall color

Author Notes: A large shade tree that often excels in dry sites and with a decent brick red fall color. Fruit litter may be a problem. It is one of the easiest oaks to transplant because of its negligible taproot.

Scientific Name: *Quercus shumardii*   Shumard Oak

Hardiness Zones: 5-9

Mature Size: 50' tall & wide in landscape; 100' tall in nature

Habit: Pyramidal to rounded

Growth Rate: Medium

Bark: Gray-brown, developing dark, deep furrows, with light gray to white scaly ridge tops

Leaf Color: Glossy dark green

Fall Color: Russet red to red; sometimes outstanding

Flowers: Catkins

Fruit: Acorn

Disease & Insect Problems: None serious

Culture: Prefers moist well-drained soils; full sun; drought and high pH tolerant

Recommended Cultivars (if any):

Author Notes: A large, lowland shade tree that is drought tolerant and readily transplantable. It is versatile with a growth habit and fall color similar to pin and scarlet oaks and suitable for planting near streams. Shumard is one of the largest southern oaks.

85

Common Name(s):

Common Sassafras

Scientific Name: *Sassafras albidum*

Hardiness Zones: 5-8

Mature Size: 30-60' tall x 25-40' wide

Habit: Pyramidal

Growth Rate: Medium-fast

Bark: Dark red-brown with deep ridges and furrows

Leaf Color: Bright green with distinctive "mitten" leaves and fragrant when crushed

Fall Color: Yellow-orange-red-purple in October; spectacular

Flowers: Yellow in April before emerging leaves; ornamental

Fruit: Dark blue drupe in September

Disease & Insect Problems: Occasional bouts of iron chlorosis in high pH soils

Culture: Ideally suited in full sun for best autumn color but will tolerate partial shade; best in moist loamy, acid, well-drained soil; prune in winter.

Recommended Cultivars (if any):

Author Notes: This attractive medium native ornamental tree has spectacular autumn color. It makes a fine specimen or excellent as a thicket in a naturalized setting. Found as single- or multi-trunked forms.

Japanese Tree Lilac

Scientific Name: *Syringa reticulata*

Hardiness Zones: 3-7

Mature Size: 20-30' tall x 15-25' wide

Habit: Upright oval becoming rounded

Growth Rate: Medium

Bark: Red-brown; similar to cherry with distinctive horizontal striping

Leaf Color: Dark green

Fall Color: Poor like most lilacs

Flowers: Showy creamy white panicles in early June; fragrant but not particularly pleasant

Fruit: Warty brown capsule not ornamental

Disease & Insect Problems: None serious including powdery mildew

Culture: Likes well-drained soil; pH adaptable; full sun for best flowering; prune after flowering

Recommended Cultivars (if any):
   'Ivory Silk'---tight crown; heavy flowerer at young age
   'Summer Snow'---rounded; flowers heavily

Author Notes: A small tree form lilac with showy early summer flowers. Considered an ornamental tree and best used as a specimen or street tree. The most trouble-free lilac available and found as single- or multi-trunked forms.

89

Littleleaf Linden

Scientific Name: *Tilia cordata*

Hardiness Zones: 3-7

Mature Size: 40-50' tall x 30' wide

Habit: Pyramidal in youth becoming rounded oval with age

Growth Rate: Medium

Bark: Gray-brown in youth becoming more rippled, furrowed, and darker

Leaf Color: Dark green, shiny, and heart-shaped

Fall Color: An uninspiring yellow-green to yellow

Flowers: Fragrant yellow-cream in late-June-early July; attracts bees

Fruit: Small nutlet

Disease & Insect Problems: Some foliage damage may occur with Japanese beetles

Culture: Ideally suited in full sun; prefers moist, well-drained soil; pH adaptable

Recommended Cultivars (if any):
    'Firecracker'---foliage appears 2 weeks later than species; yellow flower
    'Greenspire'---small white flowers; yellow fall color

Author Notes: Common large shade or specimen tree with a symmetrical shape, dense dark green foliage, and fragrant inflorescences in June-July. Initially thought to be more urban tolerant than it actually is.

Common Name(s):
Silver Linden

Scientific Name: *Tilia tomentosa*

Hardiness Zones: 4-7

Mature Size: 60' tall x 40' wide

Habit: Pyramidal in youth becoming upright oval with age

Growth Rate: Medium

Bark: Light gray in youth (like Beech) becoming gray-brown and furrowed

Leaf Color: Dark glossy green on upper surface with silver lower surface

Fall Color: Yellow

Flowers: Fragrant yellow-white in late-June-early July; attracts bees

Fruit: Small egg-shaped nutlet

Disease & Insect Problems: Some foliage damage may occur with Japanese beetles

Culture: Ideally suited in full sun; prefers moist, well-drained soil; pH adaptable; more urban tolerant than other Lindens

Recommended Cultivars (if any):
   'Wandell' (Sterling®)---broad pyramid; very disease-resistant

Author Notes: A large pyramidal shade tree tolerating heat and drought best of the Lindens. This beautiful ornamental shade tree is great for residential and golf course settings.

Scientific Name: *Ulmus americana*

American Elm

Hardiness Zones: 3-9

Mature Size: 70' tall x 40' wide

Habit: 3 distinct habits—vase-shape; oak-form; narrow form

Growth Rate: Medium-fast

Bark: Dark gray with deep broad ridges

Leaf Color: Dark glossy and lustrous

Fall Color: Typically yellow but variable

Flowers: Green-red in March and not showy

Fruit: Round samara in June and not ornamental

Disease & Insect Problems: many including Dutch elm disease, elm yellows (elm phloem necrosis), wetwood (bacterial), cankers

Culture: Prefers moist, rich soils but adaptable; full sun to partial shade; prune in fall

Recommended Cultivars (if any):

    'Jefferson'---vase-shaped; National Park Service introduction
    'New Harmony'---broad vase-shaped; U.S. National Arboretum introduction
    'Valley Forge'---classic American elm shape; most resistant of U.S. National Arboretum introductions

Author Notes: At one time used extensively as a street and large shade tree before the onslaught of Dutch elm disease. Should now use Dutch elm disease resistant (tolerant) cultivars listed above. The elm has a character (including its infamous vase-shaped form) that is very unique and graceful.

Common Name(s):
Lacebark Elm
Chinese Elm

Scientific Name: *Ulmus parviflora*

Hardiness Zones: 5-9

Mature Size: 40-50' tall & wide

Habit: Upright oval becoming rounded

Growth Rate: Medium

Bark: A magnificent mottled and exfoliating combination of green, gray, orange, and brown

Leaf Color: Shiny dark green and serrated

Fall Color: Yellow-red-purple in early to mid November

Flowers: Inconspicuous in August-September

Fruit: Samara; lime green initially turning a deep red

Disease & Insect Problems: None serious

Culture: Adaptable to extremes of soil and pH; prefers moist, well-drained fertile soils; shows excellent urban tolerance; full sun to partial sun

Recommended Cultivars (if any):

‘A. Ross Central Park’ (Central Park Splendor™)---spreading with strong wood
‘Emerald Isle’ (Athena®)---rounded; may be hardiest selection
‘Emerald Vase’ (Allee®)---upright vase shaped; smaller form of American elm
‘Ohio’---USNA introduction with reddish fall color

Author Notes: A durable large shade or specimen tree. Arguably the best all-around elm because combination of foliage, fall color, ornamental bark, and resistance to Dutch elm disease. Branch strength of this tree sometimes questioned as ice and wind storms may cause damage.

97

Scientific Name: *Ulmus x Frontier*

Hardiness Zones: 5-8

Mature Size: 40' tall x 30' wide

Habit: Oval

Growth Rate: Medium-fast

Bark: Smooth gray-green with orange lenticels

Leaf Color: Dark glossy and lustrous

Fall Color: Red-purple-burgundy

Flowers: Rarely

Fruit: None

Disease & Insect Problems: Hybrid elm exhibits both a high level of disease tolerance to Dutch elm disease, phloem necrosis, and moderate resistance to the elm leaf beetle

Culture: Prefers moist, rich soils but adaptable to poor soils; full sun; very tolerant of urban conditions and drought tolerant

Recommended Cultivars (if any):

Author Notes: A promising elm now available. A cross between *U. carpinifolia* (smooth) and *U. parviflora* (lacebark) elms, this exciting medium tree may be blazing a trail for elms in the urban landscape. It has good vigor, tolerates poor soils, grows fast, but does not get big, has small leaves and no seeds, resistant of insect and disease problems, with outstanding long fall color. The Frontier Elm tree could be on everyone's street tree list.

99

Common Name(s):

Japanese Zelkova

Scientific Name: *Zelkova serrata*

Hardiness Zones: 5-8

Mature Size: 60' tall & wide

Habit: Upright vase

Growth Rate: Medium-fast

Bark: Red-brown cherry like in youth; gray-brown with some exfoliation at maturity

Leaf Color: Dark green and serrated

Fall Color: Yellow-orange-brown with occasional hues of red-purple

Flowers: Not showy in April with leaves

Fruit: Kidney bean-shaped drupe ripening in October hidden by foliage; not showy

Disease & Insect Problems: None serious

Culture: Prefers moist, deep, well-drained soils; adaptable and shows excellent urban tolerance to heat, drought, poor soils, and varying pH; full sun to partial sun

Recommended Cultivars (if any):
   'Green Vase'---vase shaped; vigorous with upward arching branches
   'Spring Grove'---vase shaped; dark green foliage; red wine fall color
   'Village Green'---oval; wine-red fall color

Author Notes: Handsome large shade tree with vase shape, rapid growth, and stately looks. Other ornamental assets include the foliage, fine texture, and attractive bark. This is really an underutilized tree selection in today's landscapes, parks, and golf courses. It is also very tolerant of pollution and city conditions.

Canaan Fir

Scientific Name: *Abies balsamea var. phanerolepis*

Hardiness Zones: 3-8

Mature Size: 40' tall x 20-30' wide

Habit: Pyramidal

Growth Rate: Fast

Bark: Smooth and thin in youth becoming thicker and more furrowed

Leaf Color: Evergreen; deep rich green with a soft texture

Fall Color:

Flowers: Inconspicuous

Fruit: Cone

Disease & Insect Problems: None serious

Culture: Ideally suited in full sun to partial shade; prefers slightly acid, well-drained soil but has performed well in heavier (clay) soil

Recommended Cultivars (if any):

Author Notes: One of the top and most popular Christmas tree types, this fir is heat, humidity, and drought tolerant. This medium tree will grow in areas not suited for other firs. It also tolerates moist sites and late frosts. A strong candidate to be used more in landscape settings.

Scientific Name: *Juniperus virginiana*

Eastern Redcedar

Hardiness Zones: 3-9

Mature Size: 40-50' tall x 8-20' wide

Habit: Pyramidal

Growth Rate: Medium

Bark: Gray-red-brown with some exfoliation in long strips

Leaf Color: Evergreen; green to blue-green

Fall Color:

Flowers: Somewhat interesting in late winter; yellow-brown

Fruit: Cone

Disease & Insect Problems: Cedar-apple rust and bagworms

Culture: Extremely adaptable to varying adverse conditions, soil types and pH levels; seems to thrive in limestone-based soil; full sun

Recommended Cultivars (if any):

'Burkii'---pyramidal; 10-25' high; grey-blue with purple cast in winter
'Corcorcor'---upright; 25' high x 8' wide; dark green; durable
'Grey Owl'---compact; 3' high x 8' wide; substitute for Pfitzer; silver-gray

Author Notes: This medium plant is best utilized as group plantings for screens, windbreaks, or hedges. It is a very durable and tolerant evergreen where cultivars should be sought out over the species. The species will quickly naturalize in unmaintained land areas.

Scientific Name: *Metasequoia glyptostroboides*

Dawn Redwood

Hardiness Zones: 5-8

Mature Size: 70' tall x 25' wide

Habit: Conical

Growth Rate: Medium-fast

Bark: Red-brown in youth becoming darker, fissured, and exfoliating in narrow strips

Leaf Color: Deciduous; bright green

Fall Color: Cinnamon brown

Flowers: Inconspicuous

Fruit: Cone

Disease & Insect Problems: None serious

Culture: Does best in moist, deep, well-drained slightly acid soil; full sun; does not tolerate high pH soil but seems to adapt to heavy (clay) soil

Recommended Cultivars (if any):
  'Gold Rush'---gold foliage and burnt orange fall color; fast grower
  'National'---narrow conical form
  'Ogon'---yellow-green leaves and light orange bark

Author Notes: This large, stately, deciduous conifer exhibits a distinct conical form. It is a lovely specimen and ornamental tree excelling in groves, and along streams and lakes. It also makes a very effective screen.

Serbian Spruce

Scientific Name: *Picea omorika*

Hardiness Zones: 4-7

Mature Size: 50' tall x 20' wide

Habit: Pyramidal

Growth Rate: Slow-medium

Bark: Mocha brown, thin, and scaly plates

Leaf Color: Evergreen; glossy dark green

Fall Color:

Flowers: Long and attractive with a pink-red hue

Fruit: Cone

Disease & Insect Problems: Bagworms, borers, budworms, and spider mites but none serious

Culture: Best in a deep rich soil being moist and well-drained; pH adaptable; best in partial shade but tolerable to full sun; best to offer some protection from strong winter winds

Recommended Cultivars (if any):
   'Nana'---dwarf
   'Pendula'---weeping form
   'Pimiko'---rounded dwarf

Author Notes: A beautiful large evergreen specimen tree noted for its narrow, pyramidal silhouette. Graceful arching branches add to its merits. It is useful as a specimen, screen, or in groups. Here is a spruce that should be recognized and used more in the landscape.

Scientific Name: *Picea orientalis*

Hardiness Zones: 4-6

Mature Size: 55' tall x 20' wide

Habit: Pyramidal

Growth Rate: Slow

Bark: Brown with some exfoliation in thin scales

Leaf Color: Evergreen; glossy dark green

Fall Color:

Flowers: Attractive with a red hue

Fruit: Cone

Disease & Insect Problems: Mites, aphids, and bagworms but none serious

Culture: Will tolerate poor and clay soil but should be well-drained; pH adaptable; partial shade to full sun; best to offer some protection from harsh winter winds; sheltered locations offer the best sites

Recommended Cultivars (if any):
    'Atrovirens'---rich dark green needles
    'Barnes'---dwarf, nest-shape form with dark green needles
    'Skylands'---golden yellow needles

Author Notes: An attractive large evergreen specimen tree noted for its dense, narrow, habit with pendulous, horizontal branching. Here is another spruce that needs to be more readily available for use in the landscape.

Scientific Name: *Pinus bungeana*

Lacebark Pine

Hardiness Zones: 4-8

Mature Size: 30-40' tall x 20-30' wide

Habit: Pyramidal-rounded

Growth Rate: Slow…have patience

Bark: Exfoliating in patches of green, white, gray, orange, and brown; handsome

Leaf Color: Evergreen; lustrous medium to dark green

Fall Color:

Flowers: Inconspicuous

Fruit: Cone

Disease & Insect Problems: None serious

Culture: Requires well-drained soil; full sun; will tolerate slightly alkaline soils

Recommended Cultivars (if any):
'Rowe Arboretum'---exhibits more compact uniform growth habit

Author Notes: An excellent medium 4-season specimen tree valued for its showy, striking bark. It must be steadily limbed-up from a young age in order for its trunk and larger branches to receive proper sunlight which develops the mottled bark appearance. Beware that some damage may occur under heavy snowfall and ice loads on multi-trunked forms.

Eastern White Pine

Scientific Name: *Pinus strobus*

Hardiness Zones: 3-8

Mature Size: 60-80' tall x 25-40' wide

Habit: Pyramidal in youth becoming spreading

Growth Rate: Fast

Bark: Thin, smooth, gray-green in youth; darker and deeply furrowed with age

Leaf Color: Evergreen; blue-green to medium green and soft texture

Fall Color:

Flowers: Inconspicuous

Fruit: Cone

Disease & Insect Problems: White Pine blister rust and White Pine weevil

Culture: Ideally suited in moist, well-drained, acid soil but somewhat adaptable; full sun to partial shade

Recommended Cultivars (if any):

   'Fastigiata'---narrow, upright-vased columnar
   'Nana'---dwarf
   'Pendula'---weeping

Author Notes: A handsome large specimen or shade tree that also makes superb windbreaks or screens. Seasonal yellowing occurs on older needles during autumn and is normal and not indicative of any problems. Chlorosis may develop in high pH, clay soils. It is susceptible to winter salt spray (do not plant near roadways) and to strong storms which can cause broken branches.

Common Name(s):

Common Baldcypress

Scientific Name: *Taxodium distichum*

Hardiness Zones: 4-9

Mature Size: 50-70' tall x 20-30' wide

Habit: Pyramidal

Growth Rate: Medium

Bark: Red-brown and ornamentally attractive with some exfoliation

Leaf Color: Deciduous; bright yellow green in spring; sage green in summer

Fall Color: Russet-orange-bronze

Flowers: Pendulous 4" long panicles but considered ornamentally insignificant

Fruit: Cone

Disease & Insect Problems: None serious

Culture: Prefers acid, sandy soil with abundant moisture in the surface layers; adaptable to very dry or very wet sites and heavy, alkaline soil; full sun

Recommended Cultivars (if any):
   'Cascade Falls'---weeping; 8-12' tall at maturity; slow growing
   'Mickelson'---upright with finely textured foliage
   'Monarch of Illinois'---wide spreading and handsome

Author Notes: This large, deciduous conifer is an upright, stately pyramidal tree. Use as a focal point or specimen. It is superb in exceptionally moist areas where the infamous "knees" form if roots are submerged. It is also dry site capable. Some chlorosis may occur in high pH soils.

EAB—Emerald Ash Borer

As you have noticed, there are no selections of Ash (*Fraxinus sp.*) trees mentioned or recommended. The estimated 8 billion ash trees across the United States seem doomed – likely destroyed by the tiny, voracious emerald ash borer. Planting any ash specie currently poses a risk.

The emerald ash borer is a selective pest that was brought into the United States (Detroit area) from China via wooden packing crates (pallets) in 2002. The beetle is not a threat to healthy Asian ash trees but is wreaking havoc to millions of ash trees in the Midwest. In fact all 16 native ash species are at risk of infestation including their cultivars.

The native ash species make up 6% of our nation's forests. Ash trees common in the landscape-green (*F. pennsylvanica*) and white (*F. americana*) have been planted as landscape, street, and park trees in great numbers. They transplant easily, are fast growing, and very tolerant of urban growing conditions and sites. Sadly these trees were replanted to replace the American elm trees lost to Dutch elm disease. They provide shade and a statuesque appearance to any landscape.

Adults are bright emerald green with dark undersides and are very small averaging .5 inch in length. They breed within a week of emergence from $\frac{1}{8}$" diameter D-shaped exit holes on the main trunk and branches. The females lay @ 75 eggs in bark crevices in the upper third of the tree during midsummer. There the insect often remains undetected until the symptoms appear. Within a week, eggs hatch and larva immediately begin their serpentine tunneling just beneath the cork cambium. They feed on phloem (food conducting) and some xylem (water conducting) tissue. As the larva grows, so do the problems. Feeding continues until arrival of cold temperatures and the larva overwinters in a dormant mode. Pupation then begins the following April through early June with adults emerging about 2 weeks after the start of pupation. Males live 10-14 days while females live 21 days.

Larval feeding causes almost all of the injuries. The serpentine pattern of feeding can effectively girdle a branch in a single season. Most trees afflicted die because of the girdling. Symptoms of an infestation begin with chlorotic, unhealthy foliage followed by canopy decline and branch dieback. This usually occurs in the upper third of the crown. Trees often die within 3-5 years of the initial egg-laying

Humans are a significant vector of EAB by transporting infested firewood to uninfested areas. A few control measures include using the systemic insecticide imidacloprid (trade name Merit) by soil drenching or injecting into the trunk during spring. Cost of such treatments is expensive ranging from $30-$200. Studies show that a combination of larval and adult control will help slow the spread of infestation. Biological controls such as parasitic moths or wasps may one day be a viable alternative. Scientists are also working on a hybrid North American/ Asian ash tree.

A great lesson learned through this unfortunate infestation is the loss of a particular genus from overplanting practices will have an often negative and scenic impact on the landscape both in woodlots and around cities. It is always prudent to plant a variety of trees to lessen any impact that could be caused by disease or insects.

For the latest information on the status of EAB, please visit *www.emeraldashborer.info*. To preserve the American ash, early detection is the key. One has to be able to identify the emerald ash borer and the symptoms of its damage. If an infestation is detected then swift action is required to attempt to eradicate the pesty beetle. If you suspect or see any presence of EAB, immediately report the discovery to local and/or state authorities.

Expected Tree List and Reasons Why Excluded

CONIFERS

Austrian Pine (*Pinus nigra*)—Diploidia tip blight fungus

Canadian Hemlock (*Tsuga canadensis*)—needs excellent drainage and insect problems; site demanding

Colorado Blue Spruce (*Picea pungens glauca*)—overused

Douglasfir (*Pseudotsuga menziesii*)—not tolerant to dry conditions

Eastern Arborvitae (*Thuja occidentalis*)—thought of mainly as a shrub

Larch (*Larix sp.*)—does not tolerate heat (deciduous)

Norway Spruce (*Picea abies*)—overused

Scotch Pine (*Pinus sylvestris*)—Diploidia tip blight fungus

DECIDUOUS

American Beech (*Fagus grandiflora*)—compaction issues; difficult to transplant

American Hophornbeam (*Ostrya virginiana*)—difficult to find in the nursery trade

American Hornbeam (*Carpinus caroliniana*)—difficult to find in the nursery trade

American Linden or Basswood (*Tilia americana*)—bee problem and weak wood; litter

American Sweet Gum (*Liquidambar styraciflua*)—messy fruit (*gumballs*)

American Sycamore (*Platanus occidentalis*)—messy and problems with anthracnose (spring defoliation)

Bitternut Hickory (*Carya cordiformis*)—difficult to transplant thus rare in nursery trade; fruit litter

Blackhaw Viburnum (*Viburnum prunifolium*)—odorous flower and fruit; shrub

Black Locust (*Robinia pseudoacacia*)—messy and hazardous large thorns

Black Maple (*Acer nigrum*)—not commercially available

Black Walnut (*Juglans nigra*)—messy fruit; difficult to plant beds underneath

Bradford Callery Pear (*Pyrus calleryana*)—poor crotch angles; splits easily in wind storms

Bur Oak (*Quercus macrocarpa*)—tough to transplant plus has large fruit

Carolina Silverbell (*Halesia tetraptera*)—difficult to find in the nursery trade

Chinkapin Oak (*Quercus muehlenbergii*)—difficult to find in the nursery trade

Common Alder (*Alnus glutinosa*)—difficult to find in the nursery trade

Common Hackberry (*Celtis occidentalis*)—nipple gall; not common in nursery trade

Common Witchhazel (*Hamamelis virginiana*)—thought of mainly as a shrub

Eastern Cottonwood (Populus deltoides)—heavy fruiting creates litter

Hawthorns (*Crataegus sp.*)—cedar rust; thorns; messy fruit

Japanese Maple (*Acer palmatum*)—thought of more of a home landscape plant

Japanese Pagodatree (*Sophora japonica*)—messy; weak wood

Japanese Snowbell (*Styrax japonica*)—difficult to find; marginally hardy

Japanese Stewartia (*Stewartia japonica*)—fragile; prefers PM shade and acidic, moist, well-drained soil

Katsura Tree (*Cercidiphyllum japonicum*)—difficult to find; slow to establish; need much water when young

London Planetree (*Platanus x acerifolia*)—messy

Northern Catalpa (*Catalpa speciosa*)—messy and catalpa worms

Norway Maple (*Acer platanoides*)—provides dense shade making growing grass difficult; surface roots

Ohio Buckeye (*Aesculus glabra*)—messy; defoliates by end of summer

Osage Orange (*Maclura pomifera*)—messy with hazardous large fruit; thorny branches

Paper Birch (*Betula papyrifera*)—bronze birch borer

Saucer Magnolia (*Magnolia x soulangiana*)—total flower loss from late spring freezes

Scarlet Oak (*Quercus coccinea*)—difficult to find in the nursery trade

Shagbark Hickory (Carya ovata)—difficult to transplant thus rare in nursery trade; fruit litter

Silver Maple (*Acer saccharinum*)—weak wood and poor crotch angles

White Oak (*Quercus alba*)—difficult to transplant; nursery production is slow

Wild Black Cherry (*Prunus serotina*)—constant battle with tent caterpillars; messy fruit

Willow (*Salix alba*)—weak wood and messy; short-lived

Scientific Name Plant Usage Guides

Trees Considered Small-Sized

Acer buergerianum
Acer griseum
Aesculus parviflora
Aesculus pavia
Amelanchier sp.
Cercis canadensis
Chionanthus virginicus
Cornus florida
Cornus kousa
Cornus mas
Magnolia stellata
Magnolia virginiana
Malus sp.
Parrotia persica
Syringa reticulata

Trees Considered Medium-Sized

Abies balsamea var. phanerolepis
Acer rubrum
Carpinus betulus
Cladrastis kentuckea
Juniperus virginiana
Koelreuteria paniculata
Pinus bungeana
Sassafras albidum
Ulmus x Frontier

Trees Considered Large-Sized

Acer sacharrum
Aesculus octandra

Betula nigra
Fagus sylvatica
Ginkgo biloba
Gleditsia triacanthos var. inermis
Gymnocladus dioicus
Liriodendron tulipifera
Magnolia acuminata
Metasequoia glyptostroboides
Nyssa sylvatica
Picea omorika
Picea orientalis
Pinus strobus
Quercus acutissima
Quercus bicolor
Quercus imbricaria
Quercus palustris
Quercus rubra
Quercus shumardii
Taxodium distichum
Tilia cordata
Tilia tomentosa
Ulmus americana
Ulmus parviflora
Zelkova serrata

Trees for Dry Areas

Abies balsamea var. phanerolepis
Cladrastis kentuckea
Ginkgo biloba
Gleditsia triacanthos var. inermis
Juniperus virginiana
Koelreuteria paniculata
Malus sp.
Pinus strobus
Quercus rubra
Quercus imbricaria
Tilia tomentosa

Trees for Wet Areas *Generally suited for areas prone to occasional flooding and/or ponding of water such as streambanks, low areas, etc.

Acer rubrum

Amelanchier sp.

Betulus nigra

Gleditsia triacanthos var. inermis

Magnolia virginiana

Metasequoia glyptostroboides

Nyssa sylvatica

Quercus bicolor

Quercus palustris

Quercus shumardii

Taxodium distichum

Tilia tomentosa

Ulmus americana

Trees for 4 Season Appeal

Acer griseum

Amelanchier sp.

Betulus nigra

Cornus florida

Cornus kousa

Fagus sylvatica

Parrotia persica

Pinus bungeana

Trees for Spring Flowers

Aesculus octandra

Aesculus pavia

Amelanchier sp.

Cercis canadensis

Chionanthus virginicus

Cladrastis kentuckea

Cornus florida

Cornus kousa

Cornus mas

Liriodenron tulipifera

Magnolia acuminata

Magnolia stellata

Malus sp.

Sassafras albidum

Trees for Summer Flowering

Aesculus parviflora
Koelreuteria paniculata
Magnolia virginiana
Tilia cordata
Tilia tomentosa

Trees for Fall Color

Acer buergerianum
Acer griseum
Acer rubrum
Acer saccharum
Amelanchier sp.
Betulus nigra
Cladrastis kentuckea
Cornus florida
Cornus kousa
Ginkgo biloba
Gleditsia triacanthos var. inermis
Liriodenron tulipifera
Magnolia acuminata
Metasequoia glyptostroboides
Nyssa sylvatica
Parrotia persica
Quercus palustris
Quercus shumardii
Sassafras albidum
Taxodium distichum
Ulmus parviflora
Ulmus x Frontier

Trees for Winter Interest

Acer buergerianum (Bark)
Acer griseum (Bark)
Amelanchier sp. (Bark)
Betulus nigra (Bark)
Fagus sylvatica (Bark)
Gymnocladus doicus (Texture)
Malus sp. (Fruit)
Pinus bungeana (Bark)
Quercus bicolor (Texture)

Trees for Ornamental Bark

Acer buergerianum

Acer griseum

Amelanchier sp.

Betulus nigra

Carpinus betulus

Fagus sylvatica

Metasequoia glyptostroboides

Parrotia persica

Pinus bungeana

Taxodium distichum

Ulmus parviflora

Zelkova serrata

Trees Considered to Be Ornamental *Generally considered ornamental if under 25' and having 1 or more ornamental aspects.

Acer griseum

Amelanchier sp.

Betulus nigra

Cercis canadensis

Cladrastis kentuckea

Cornus kousa

Cornus mas

Koelreuteria paniculata

Magnolia stellata

Magnolia virginiana

Malus sp.

Parrotia persica

Syringa reticulata

Trees with Ornamental Fruit

Amelanchier sp.

Chionanthus virginicus

Cornus florida

Cornus mas

Malus sp.

Magnolia acuminata

Magnolia virginiana

Nyssa sylvatica

Sassafras albidum

Trees Considered to be Specimens

Acer griseum
Acer rubrum (Cultivars)
Aesculus pavia
Amelanchier sp.
Chionanthus virginicus
Cornus florida
Cornus kousa
Cornus mas
Fagus sylvatica
Ginkgo biloba
Magnolia stellata
Malus sp.
Metasequoia glyptostroboides
Nyssa sylvatica
Parrotia persica
Picea omorika
Picea orientalis
Pinus bungeana
Pinus strobus
Sassafras albidum
Syringa reticulata
Taxodium distichum
Tilia cordata
Ulmus parviflora

Trees Tolerant of Partial Shade

Aesculus parviflora
Amelanchier sp.
Cercis canadensis
Chionanthus virginicus
Cornus florida
Cornus mas
Magnolia virginiana
Parrotia persica
Picea omorika
Picea orientalis
Sassafras albidum

Trees for Shade Effect

Acer buergerianum

Acer rubrum

Acer saccharum

Betulus nigra

Fagus sylvatica

Ginkgo biloba

Koelreuteria paniculata

Magnolia acuminata

Nyssa sylvatica

Pinus strobus

Quercus acutissima

Quercus imbricaria

Quercus palustris

Quercus rubra

Quercus shumardii

Tilia cordata

Tilia tomentosa

Ulmus americana

Zelkova serrata

Trees Tolerant of Salt Spray

Amelanchier sp.

Gleditsia triacanthos var. inermis

Juniperus virginiana

Nyssa sylvatica

Tilia cordata

Trees for Screens

Amelanchier sp.

Carpinus betulus

Cornus mas

Juniperus virginiana

Metasequoia glyptostroboides

Picea omorika

Pinus strobus

Sassafras albidum

Trees for Urban Settings

Carpinus betulus

Gingko biloba

Gleditsia triacanthos var. inermis

Juniperus virginiana

Koelreuteria paniculata

Parrotia persica

Quercus palustris

Quercus rubra

Tilia tomentosa

Ulmus parviflora

Ulmus x Frontier

Zelkova serrata

Trees Tolerant of High pH Soils

Acer griseum

Acer saccharum

Aesculus parviflora

Aesculus pavia

Amelanchier sp.

Carpinus betulus

Cercis canadensis

Cladrastis kentuckea

Cornus mas

Ginkgo biloba

Gleditsia triacanthos var. inermis

Gymnocladus dioicus

Juniperus virginiana

Koelreuteria paniculata

Magnolia acuminata

Magnolia stellata

Malus sp.

Parrotia persica

Syringa reticulata

Taxodium distichum

Tilia cordata

Tilia tomentosa

Ulmus x Frontier

Common Name Plant Usage Guides

Trees Considered Small-Sized
 Bottlebrush Buckeye
 Corneliancherry Dogwood
 Eastern Redbud
 Flowering Crabapple
 Flowering Dogwood
 Japanese Tree Lilac
 Kousa Dogwood
 Paperbark Maple
 Persian Parrotia
 Red Buckeye
 Serviceberry
 Star Magnolia
 Sweetbay Magnolia
 Trident Maple
 White Fringetree

Trees Considered Medium-Sized
 American Yellowwood
 Canaan Fir
 Common Sassafras
 Eastern Redcedar
 European Hornbeam
 Frontier Elm
 Lacebark Pine
 Panicled Goldenraintree
 Red Maple

Trees Considered Large-Sized
 American Elm
 Black Tupelo

Common Baldcypress
Cucumbertree Magnolia
Dawn Redwood
Eastern White Pine
European Beech
Ginkgo
Honey Locust
Japanese Zelkova
Kentucky Coffeetree
Lacebark Elm
Littleleaf Linden
Oriental Spruce
Pin Oak
Red Oak
River Birch
Sawtooth Oak
Serbian Spruce
Shingle Oak
Shumard Oak
Silver Linden
Sugar Maple
Swamp White Oak
Tuliptree
Yellow Buckeye

Trees for Dry Areas

American Yellowwood
Canaan Fir
Eastern Redcedar
Eastern White Pine
Flowering Crabapple
Ginkgo
Panicled Goldenraintree
Red Oak
Shingle Oak
Silver Linden
Thornless Honeylocust

Trees for Wet Areas *Generally suited for areas prone to occasional flooding and/or ponding of water such as streambanks, low areas, etc.

American Elm
Black Tupelo
Common Baldcypress
Dawn Redwood
Pin Oak
Red Maple
River Birch
Serviceberry
Shumard Oak
Silver Linden
Swamp White Oak
Sweetbay Magnolia
Thornless Honeylocust

Trees for 4 Season Appeal

European Beech
Flowering Dogwood
Kousa Dogwood
Lacebark Pine
Paperbark Maple
Persian Parrotia
River Birch
Serviceberry

Trees for Spring Flowers

American Yellowwood
Common Sassafras
Corneliancherry Dogwood
Cucumbertree Magnolia
Eastern Redbud
Flowering Crabapple
Flowering Dogwood
Kousa Dogwood
Red Buckeye
Serviceberry
Star Magnolia
Tuliptree
White Fringetree
Yellow Buckeye

Trees for Summer Flowering
Bottlebrush Buckeye
Littleleaf Linden
Panicled Goldenraintree
Silver Linden
Sweetbay Magnolia

Trees for Fall Color
American Yellowwood
Black Tupelo
Common Baldcypress
Common Sassafras
Dawn Redwood
Flowering Dogwood
Frontier Elm
Ginkgo
Kousa Dogwood
Lacebark Elm
Paperbark Maple
Persian Parrotia
Pin Oak
Red Maple
River Birch
Serviceberry
Shumard Oak
Sugar Maple
Thornless Honeylocust
Trident Maple
Tuliptree
Yellow Buckeye

Trees for Winter Interest
Crabapple (Fruit)
European Beech (Bark)
Kentucky Coffeetree (Texture)
Lacebark Pine (Bark)
Paperbark Maple (Bark)
River Birch (Bark)
Swamp White Oak (Texture)
Serviceberry (Bark)
Trident Maple (Bark)

Trees for Ornamental Bark

Common Baldcypress
Dawn Redwood
European Beech
European Hornbeam
Japanese Zelkova
Lacebark Elm
Lacebark Pine
Paperbark Maple
Persian Parrotia
River Birch
Serviceberry
Trident Maple

Trees Considered to Be Ornamental *Generally considered ornamental if under 25' and having 1 or more ornamental aspects.

American Yellowwood
Corneliancherry Dogwood
Eastern Redbud
Flowering Crabapple
Japanese Tree Lilac
Kousa Dogwood
Panicled Goldenraintree
Paperbark Maple
Persian Parrotia
River Birch
Serviceberry
Star Magnolia
Sweetbay Magnolia

Trees with Ornamental Fruit

Black Tupelo
Common Sassafras
Corneliancherry Dogwood
Cucumbertree Magnolia
Flowering Crabapple
Flowering Dogwood
Serviceberry
Sweetbay Magnolia
White Fringetree

Trees Considered to Be Specimens

Black Tupelo
Common Baldcypress
Common Sassafras
Corneliancherry Dogwood
Dawn Redwood
Eastern White Pine
European Beech
Flowering Crabapple
Flowering Dogwood
Ginkgo
Japanese Tree Lilac
Kousa Dogwood
Lacebark Elm
Lacebark Pine
Littleleaf Linden
Oriental Spruce
Paperbark Maple
Persian Parrotia
Red Buckeye
Red Maple (Cultivars)
Serbian Spruce
Serviceberry
Star Magnolia
White Fringetree

Trees Tolerant of Partial Shade

Bottlebrush Buckeye
Common Sassafras
Corneliancherry Dogwood
Eastern Redbud
Flowering Dogwood
Oriental Spruce
Persian Parrotia
Serbian Spruce
Serviceberry
Sweetbay Magnolia
White Fringetree

Trees for Shade Effect

American Elm
Black Tupelo
Cucumbertree Magnolia
Eastern White Pine
European Beech
Ginkgo
Japanese Zelkova
Littleleaf Linden
Panicled Goldenraintree
Pin Oak
Red Maple
Red Oak
River Birch
Sawtooth Oak
Shingle Oak
Shumard Oak
Sugar Maple
Trident Maple
Yellow Buckeye

Trees Tolerant of Salt Spray

Black Tupelo
Eastern Redcedar
Honey Locust
Littleleaf Linden
Serviceberry

Trees for Screens

Common Sassafras
Corneliancherry Dogwood
Dawn Redwood
Eastern Redcedar
Eastern White Pine
European Hornbeam
Serbian Spruce
Serviceberry

Trees for Urban Settings

Eastern Redcedar
European Hornbeam
Frontier Elm
Ginkgo
Japanese Zelkova
Lacebark Elm
Panicled Goldenraintree
Persian Parrotia
Pin Oak
Red Oak
Silver Linden
Thornless Honeylocust

Trees Tolerant of High pH Soils

American Yellowwood
Bottlebrush Buckeye
Common Baldcypress
Corneliancherry Dogwood
Cucumbertree Magnolia
Eastern Redbud
Eastern Redcedar
European Hornbeam
Flowering Crabapple
Frontier Elm
Ginkgo
Japanese Tree Lilac
Kentucky Coffeetree
Littleleaf Linden
Panicled Goldenraintree
Paperbark Maple
Persian Parrotia
Red Buckeye
Serviceberry
Silver Linden
Star Magnolia
Sugar Maple
Thornless Honeylocust

United States Hardiness Zone Map

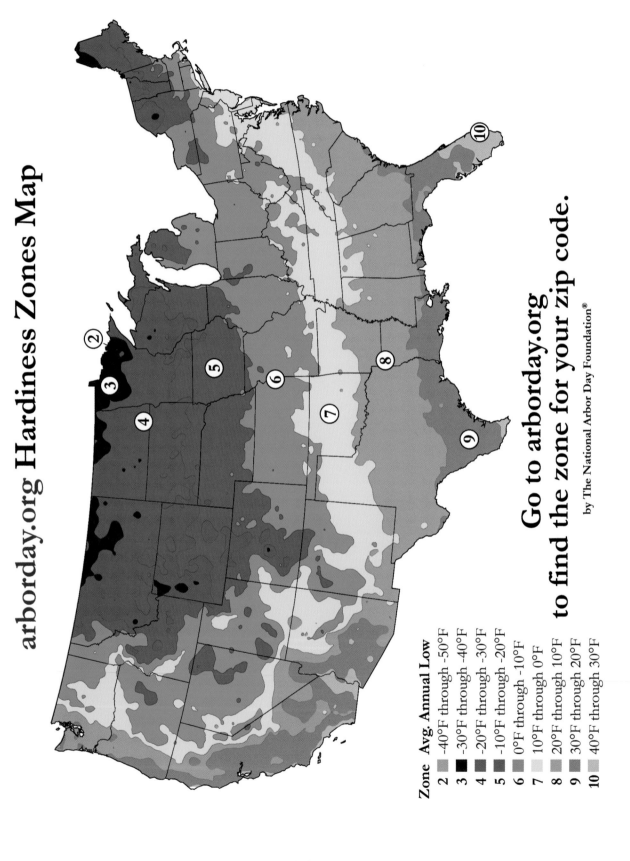

arborday.org Hardiness Zones Map

Go to arborday.org
to find the zone for your zip code.

by The National Arbor Day Foundation®

Zone	Avg. Annual Low
2	-40°F through -50°F
3	-30°F through -40°F
4	-20°F through -30°F
5	-10°F through -20°F
6	0°F through -10°F
7	10°F through 0°F
8	20°F through 10°F
9	30°F through 20°F
10	40°F through 30°F

Arborday.org Hardiness Zones
Alaska and Hawaii

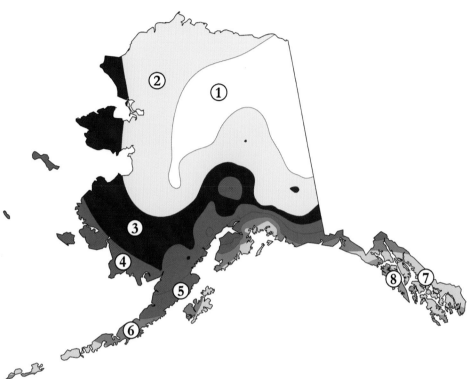

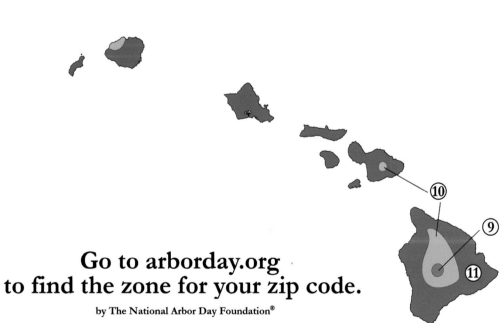

Zone	Avg. Annual Low
1	Below -50°F
2	-40°F through -50°F
3	-30°F through -40°F
4	-20°F through -30°F
5	-10°F through -20°F
6	0°F through -10°F
7	10°F through 0°F
8	20°F through 10°F
9	30°F through 20°F
10	40°F through 30°F
11	Above 40°F

Go to arborday.org
to find the zone for your zip code.

by The National Arbor Day Foundation®

Bibliography–Literature Cited–References

Books

Dirr, M.A. *Manual of Woody Landscape Plants*, 5th ed. Stipes Publishing, Champaign, IL, 1998.

Hurdzan, M.J. *Golf Course Architecture,* Sleeping Bear Press, Chelsea, MI, 1996.

Lilly, S. *Golf Course Tree Management,* Ann Arbor Press, Chelsea, MI, 1999.

Sydnor, T.D., K. Smith and R. Heiligmann, *Ash Replacements for Urban and Woodland Plantings*, The Ohio State University Extension Bulletin 924, Columbus, OH, 2005.

Sydnor, T.D. and W.F. Cowen, *Ohio Trees*, The Ohio State University Extension Bulletin 700, Columbus, OH, 2000.

Magazines

Backyard Living

Fine Gardening

Golf Journal

Horticulture

The American Gardener

Tree Services

Turf Central

Newspaper

The Columbus Dispatch

Websites

ArborCom *www.arborcom.ca*

Golf Course Superintendents Association of America *www.gcsaa.org*

Ohio State University Plantfacts *www.plantfacts.osu.edu*

United States Golf Association *www.usga.org*

Index

Scientific names are displayed in italicized type,
common names in **bold** type